Touched by God

Original Poems by

Mary Lou Greenwood Snyder

CONTENTS

FOREWORD

Poetry is the expression of feelings and ideas that reveal the heart and soul of the poet while touching the heart and soul of the reader. Those who know Mary Lou best, her husband and children, share their thoughts on this collection of poems.

๛

During our 59 years of marriage, my wife has written these poems and the words are from her heart. She takes immense pleasure in putting her thoughts into words, and her words into poems. She loves them dearly, as I do her.

Barry

๛

Mom, your words are an inspirational expression of kindness, love, and faith for all to hear and feel! Love you always.

Brian

๛

Calming, kindness, peace of heart. Enduring words of emotion and healing, in which I have found great comfort. Love you, mom. Thanks for being you.

David

‰

Mother, you shine brighter than the sun. From one poet to another, my original lyrics from Mystic Miner: "Punch your head through the sky, down through the clouds. Give him a helping hand, you know how. Help him up to his feet, help him up in his mind..."

Steve

‰

Mom, your beautiful poems reveal the essence of your being. Thank you for sharing your heart and faith with us. I'm proud of you and I love you.

Carol

‰

To my mother, the one whose grounded me and always been there to keep me on the right path in life with God, my family, and myself. Thank you.

Kenneth

INTRODUCTION

These poems were written over the years, inspired by my faith in God and the deepest feelings within my heart. God is truly my best friend. I pray to him every day that he will work through us, speak through us, touch through us, help through us, and love through us. I hope you find a connection with God and are inspired by these poems.

~ Mary Lou Greenwood Snyder

Touched by God

Peace

Peace is a moment of stillness. Peace is watching soft billowy clouds moving across the clear blue sky, water glistening in the golden sunlight.

Seeing the majesty of mountains standing against the horizon, watching the snow falling gently, silently to the ground. Peace is truly all around.

Lord, we feel the gentleness of you in a soft summer breeze and the strength of you in the wind. You give us life and all good things, but still the evilness of man spreads like disease across the land, causing sorrow and great strife, making misery out of life.

Lord, give us faith, peace of mind, healthy bodies, and happy times. Let us not go astray, we need you Lord, every day. Peace is what we're searching for, why do we want so much more? Just look to God, it can be found. Peace is truly all around.

Memories

How I love to wander back,
through the memories of my past.
It all seems so long ago,
but through the years we all must go.

Being a child was so free,
running through meadows, climbing in trees,
picking wild flowers, sitting by streams,
catching frogs, and dreaming dreams.

We all must leave our youth behind,
to only grow older and older with time.
But I know that dying will be,
a most wondrous journey taken by me.

My soul will leave my body behind,
floating through paradise off into time.
Through the clouds in heaven I'll be,
at peace with God for eternity.

I Had a Vision

I had a vision, do you know what it was?

There was God, there was man, there was heaven above.

God spoke to the man and took from his side,

a piece of his rib and gave him a bride.

God said to the woman, "Now this is your man.

It is meant that you walk side-by-side, hand-in-hand.

Don't take each other for granted, it's easy to do.

Just ask that I bless you and let you be you."

Prayer of a Housewife

Understanding myself wasn't easy for me,
there was so much more I wanted to be.
Housework seems such drudgery,
it swallows up so much of me.

The kids take up so much of my time.
I love them dearly, but why can't they mind?

Being a mother and being a wife
wasn't all I wanted from life.
One day you're up, the next you're down,
what is it in me that wants to be found?

One day as I knelt to pray,
the Lord touched me in a special way,
"Woman, face your life with faith and hope
and you will find that you can cope.
For being a mother and being a wife
isn't always an easy life,
but one that I have chosen for you
and one that I will see you through.
And because you knelt to pray,
I'll bless you in a special way."

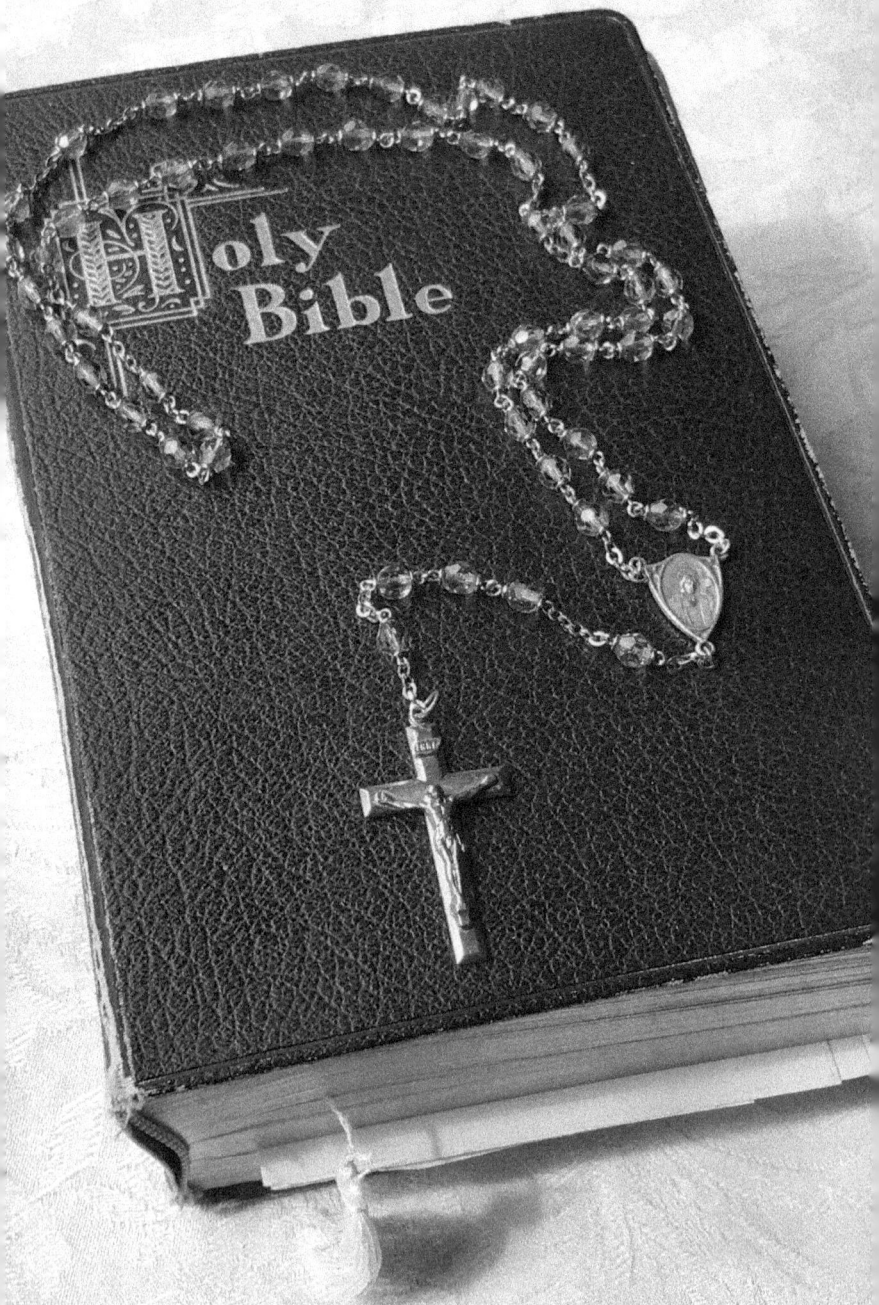

Heal My Wounds

Oh God, from you I cannot hide
the hurt, the pain, I feel inside.
And so I'm asking you today,
to help me in a special way.

I need to know that you are there;
I need to know that someone cares.
Sometimes we stray from your path,
and only you can bring us back.

My Best Friend

Alone I shall never be,
God is always here with me.
He helps me through each new day,
all I have to do is pray.

God's healing powers from above,
touch my heart with his great love.
His holy spirit is here to stay,
guiding me along the way.

God is really my best friend,
with him life will never end!

Happy Homemaker

I'm happy to be a mother, a wife,
I'm happy I chose this way of life.

I'm happy God gave me children to love.
I'm happy God cares for me from above.

Here in my home where I want to be,
I'm loving and caring for those closest to me.

No greater reward could I wish as a wife,
than be happily married to one man for life.

Life

Tiny fingers, tiny toes,
two eyes, and a little nose.
Growing up inside of me,
and one day will come to be.

A man, a woman on their own,
trying to make this earth their home.
Trying to find their place in life,
through all the pain and all the strife.

At the end, we hope will be
Heaven
God
Tranquility
All our loved ones, you and me.

My Husband

When I think of love, I think of you,
and all you say, and all you do.

I knew one day I'd be your bride,
and felt all warm and good inside.

As I stood there dressed in lace,
I felt God's touch through your embrace.

Happy Anniversary

To my husband of sixteen years,
through the happiness and the tears,
through the highs and through the lows,
I pray our love only grows.

May God Bless the years ahead,
and let us remember the vows we said.

As we stood side-by-side
on the day I became your bride,
I prayed to God from my heart,
the two of us would never part.

The Crown

Liberated I am not, when hubby's home he calls the shots. When he is out, I wear the crown. When he comes in, I just step down.

Oh, How I've Changed!

Housework can be such drudgery,
it takes up so much energy.

When I first became a bride,
I did my work with so much pride.

The years have passed, the kids have grown,
soon they will be on their own.

How unimportant it all seems,
to clean the house and sew up seams.

I'm older now, the house can wait,
I'm going out to celebrate!

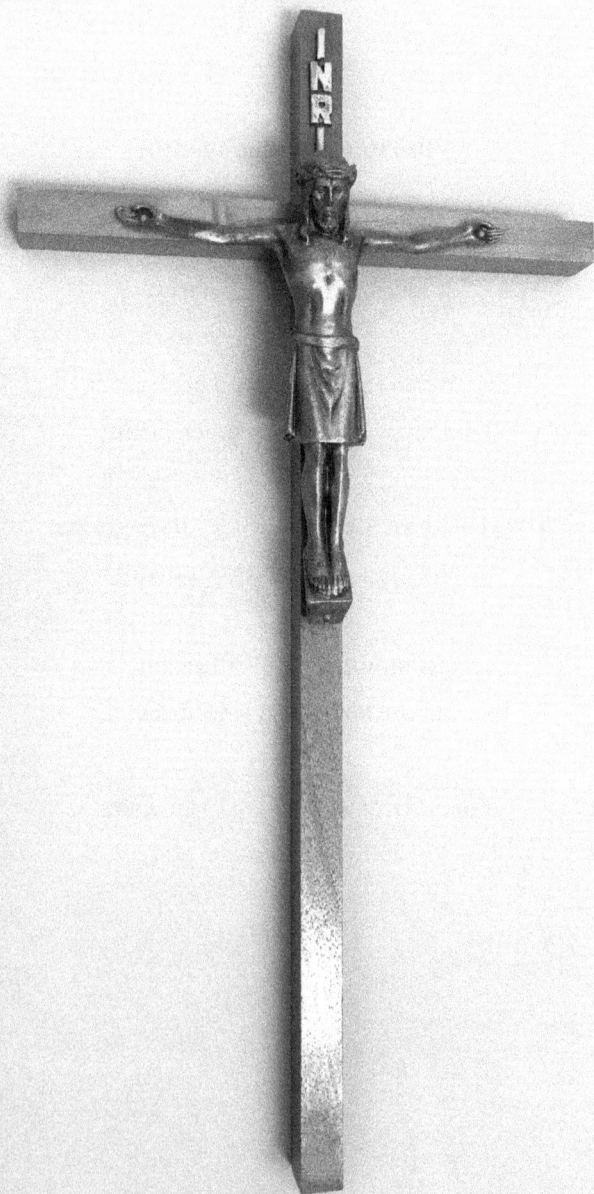

Proving Ground

Life is a proving ground for our souls,
may God be with us as we go.

Touch through us, speak through us as we roam,
until the day you bring us home.

Thanking God every day,
as we work and as we play.

Doing the best that we can,
always lending a helping hand.

The day will come we're laid to rest,
I pray we will have done our best.

Amen

Going Home

In the silence of the night,
I'm ascending toward God's Holy Light.

Now my life on earth is done,
I will meet God's only son.

Where I'll dwell for eternity
with the Holy Trinity
Father
Son
Holy Ghost
It is to you we lift this host.

Thank you Lord for all you do.
Thank you Lord for seeing me through.

May God bless and watch over you
until he brings you home.

Believe

Look outside, you can see a touch of God in every tree, in the sun and in the moon, and in the flowers as they bloom, in the animals as they play and work so hard to find their way.

God gave us everything to exist, just take a moment as you sit out in the sun that warms the earth, and you too will feel the might of the one who has to fight to keep our souls for his own when evilness surrounds us.

Oh how can we be so blind, to turn from God's love all the time? Just ask God to make you strong, he will never let you down.

How can we doubt that there is God? Can we doubt that there is man? Why is it so hard to understand? Why is it so hard to see God's plan?

Pray to God every day, he will help you find your way. Call out to God and you will see that you too will soon believe.

NOTES FROM THE POET

"*Memories*" is one of my favorite poems. I had a good childhood. I am so grateful that I had a wonderful mother and father who loved us, worked hard for us, and cared for us.

"*Peace*" was written in the 1970s. The kids were at school. I was sitting outside in my yard in Rochester, Michigan. I was looking at the sky, talking to God, and enjoying the beauty of all his creations.

"*I Had a Vision*" captures the essence of my heart. It's what I believe should be the foundation of a relationship between a man and a woman as they become husband and wife.

I had just written "*Proving Ground*" when, one day in church, the priest began his sermon with, "Why are you here? I'm a mess. You're a mess. We're all a mess." I thought, "I'm here because God put me here and life is a proving ground for our souls." I wanted to raise my hand and recite my poem, but I didn't.

"*Believe*" is another one of my favorite poems. Man has not created anything that can compare with what God has created. May the honor and the glory always go to God.

ABOUT THE POET

Mary Lou was born in 1938 in Breitung Township, Michigan (near Iron Mountain) in a little house on a hill, right next door to her grandfather's house. At the age of two, she moved with her family to Detroit. They lived in a modest six-flat until she was ten, when they moved into a home her father built in East Detroit. Her father, Joseph Lloyd, worked for the Packard Motor Car Company and her mother, Elida, was a homemaker. She has three brothers, Lloyd, Jerry (stillborn), and Robert.

Mary Lou remembers her mother singing religious songs and talking about Jesus. Her mother was Lutheran prior to converting to Catholicism. Her paternal grandmother was a devout Catholic. Her maternal grandmother read the bible every night and attended a Lutheran church regularly.

When Mary Lou was a young girl, she walked to St. Veronica Parish in East Detroit where she bought herself a bible, which she still reads from today. Mary Lou has been a Catholic Eucharistic Minister for many years and enjoys attending church. However, she believes that your own personal relationship with God is what matters most.

Mary Lou currently lives with her husband, Barry, in Clarkston, Michigan. They were high school sweethearts and have been married since 1961. They have five children, a son-in-law, three daughters-in-law, and seven grandchildren.

Mary Lou and Barry on their wedding day. May 6th, 1961

Mary Lou and Barry's 50th anniversary celebration.
Mackinac Island, Michigan, May 2011

From left to right.
First row: Jessica, Olivia
Second Row: Ian, Mary Lou, Mallory, Barry, Ivan
Third Row, each end: Barry, Calvin
Back: Michelle, David, Kassia, Brian, Carol, Dave,
Kenneth, Jenni, Steven

www.ingramcontent.com/pod-product-compliance
Lightning Source LLC
Chambersburg PA
CBHW032115040426
42337CB00041B/1333